Contents

An 1804 watercolour, thought to be of Jane Austen, by her sister Cassandra.

Introduction

Harlestone Park, Northamptonshire, a Repton-designed Georgian country house of a style very familar to Jane.

Jane Austen remains one of the most influential novelists in the English language. Her canon of work is the six major novels which continue to be read, discussed, studied, translated and adapted for film and television. Jane Austen societies exist worldwide, whilst the locations she was connected to remain places of pilgrimage and her admirers over the years have been legionary.

'That young lady had a talent for describing the involvements of feelings and characters of ordinary life, which is to me the most wonderful I ever met with.' So said Walter Scott. The compliment was returned in *Persuasion* where one of Scott's works is praised. Samuel Taylor Coleridge, Sydney Smith and Robert Southey were also admirers of Austen's work, although there have been some famous detractors. Charlotte Brontë was critical:

'What sees keenly, speaks aptly, moves flexibly, it suits her to study: but what throbs fast and full, though hidden, what the blood rushes through, what is the unseen seat of life and the sentient target of death – this Miss Austen ignores' while Mark Twain had this to say: 'Jane Austen? Why, I go so far as to say that any library is a good library that does not contain a volume by Jane Austen. Even if it contains no other book.'

Austen's work has been continually adapted over the years for both cinema and television, although again not everyone is in favour. 'Seeing a movie or television adaptation of any of Jane Austen's works is like hearing a symphony of Mozart played on a harmonica' is a sentiment once expressed on Swedish television. Notwithstanding, it may come as no surprise to learn that *Pride and Prejudice* is the novel which has been adapted more times than any other. Film buffs may also be interested to know that in one such adapatation, Mr Collins' profession was changed to a librarian.

Jane Austen: A Literary Challenge is intended to have a broad appeal; those versed in all things Austenian are not the sole audience. Families, students, teachers, librarians, book groups, those who belong to quiz teams and those who don't – all are invited to use and enjoy this book. To this end, questions have been graded into four levels: from easy via medium and difficult to those requiring more complicated research.

Picture questions, multiple choice questions and those which simply require a 'true' or 'false' answer will all be found inside, together with those questions which may prove more challenging. At the back of the book, the answers are provided separately.

Perhaps it is worth mentioning that reading this introduction may help you to answer one or two questions.

The book has been divided into various sections, some general, others specific. You will therefore find 'Courtships, Weddings and Marriages',

JANE AUSTEN

A LITERARY CHALLENGE

Helen Barton

BartonBooks

First published in 2009 by BartonBooks

BartonBooks

Copyright © Helen Barton 2009

ISBN   978-0-9527257-5-6

Typeset and designed by Bookcraft, Stroud, Gloucestershire
Printed and bound in the UK by The Dorset Press, Dorchester

The Abbey Gate School in Reading, which Jane and her sister Cassandra attended in 1784.

Chawton House and School from a painting of about 1809. Jane's brother owned Chawton House and Jane's mother and her sister Cassandra are buried in the churchyard.

'*Sitting under trees with Fanny*', *an illustration by Hugh Thomson from* Mansfield Park.

together with 'Locations and Buildings' and 'Jane Austen, her Family, her Life and Times' alongside specific sets of questions on each of the major novels.

The intention of this book is to provide an entertaining approach to Austen, her life and work. If you consider yourself to be one of the greatest living experts on *Persuasion* or *Northanger Abbey,* I hope you will enjoy this book alongside the Austen newcomer. Whoever you are, I am sure none of you will be asking the following: 'So she wouldn't be available for book signings?' a question allegedly asked by an American network executive when told that *Pride and Prejudice* was published in 1813.

Dixon's 'View of Bath', 1822. Many of the landmarks in this landscape would have been familiar to Jane.

Jane Austen, her Family, her Life and Times

1 How many major novels did Jane Austen write?

2 All the heroines in Austen's novels are finally married. True or false?

3 What was Jane's father called?

4 What was his profession?

5 Where was Jane Austen born?
(a) Worcestershire   (b) Kent   (c) Hampshire

6 How many times did Jane Austen marry?

7 Jane's mother was called Emma. True or false?

8 How many years did Jane live at Chawton?
(a) 5   (b) 8   (c) 17

9 With which European country was England at war during Jane's lifetime?

10 What is a landau?

11 For most of Jane Austen's life, who was the Prime Minister?

12 In which of these periods did Jane Austen live?
(a) Victorian   (b) Georgian   (c) Edwardian

13 Jane Austen had two sisters. True or false?

14 Name the two revolutions that took place during Austen's lifetime.

15 The hats shown below were popular in the early nineteenth century. Put them in chronological order.

    A   B   C

16 Which king was on the throne during Jane's lifetime?

17 What was Jane Austen called at home?
(a) Jenny   (b) Janey   (c) Susan

18 How many of the novels were published during Jane's lifetime?
(a) six   (b) none   (c) four

Jane Austen, her Family, her Life and Times

1 Were any of Jane's novels published anonymously and, if so, how many?

2 What was the relationship between Jane and James Edward Austen-Leigh?

3 Two of Jane's brothers had the same career? What was it?

4 Which musical instrument did Jane play?

5 There were only two times when Jane lived away from home. Where did she live and why?

6 Name as many of Jane's brothers as you can.

7 How many years did Jane live in Hampshire?
(a) 25   (b) 17   (c) 11

8 The Austen family moved when Jane's father retired. Where did they go?

9 What is the significance of College Street, Winchester?

10 Who destroyed Jane's letters?

11   Name the material that the gowns shown below were made from.

12   They had a classical influence. What was it?

13   'Her voice was extremely sweet. She delivered herself with fluency and precision.' Identify both the subject and the author.

14   What was a 'Mameluke cap'?

15   What was a reticule?

16   What is the significance of the words 'By a Lady'?

DIFFICULT   *Jane Austen, her Family, her Life and Times*

1 What were the main two architectural styles of architecture in the Regency period?

2 Who was the eldest daughter of Jane's brother James?

3 Who is speaking about Jane's life? 'of events her life was singularly barren: few changes and no great crises ever broke the smooth current of its course ...'

4 Jane earned some money from *Sense and Sensibility*. How much?

5 In the context of the church and the clergy, what was pluralism?

6 What was a hack chaise?

7 The disease Jane died of is now known as what?

8 Where and when was Jane's funeral held?

9 What is the significance of the poet Cowper?

10 A member of Jane's family wrote the extract below. Who was it?

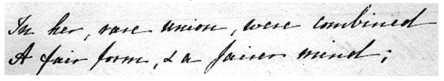

11 Name the church where Jane's father is buried

12 In which month and year were Jane's parents married?

13 The Austens were particularly close to three families.
Name as many as you can.

14 'He is a very gentlemanlike, good looking, pleasant young man,
I assure you.' This is taken from one of Jane Austen's letters but
who is she referring to?

15 What is the name of the jackets in the pictures below?

16 Why were reticules used at this time?

17 'She openeth her mouth with wisdom and in her tongue is the law
of kindness'. Where would you find these words?

18 'Sir, I have in my possession a manuscript novel, …' George Austen
wrote this in a letter to a London publisher. To which novel is he referring?

19 What was the publisher's name?

Jane Austen, her Family, her Life and Times

1 In which year did Jane move to Chawton?

2 'I don't think her superb intelligence brought her happiness.'
Who said this of Jane Austen?

3 Mary Wollstonecraft's most well-known work was published in 1792.
What was it called?

4 One of Jane's brothers had a branch bank in Alton.
What was its address?

5 Why is the date 18 March 1817 significant?

6 Who lived at Wyards?

7 Name the person who wrote the following to Thomas Egerton in
1811 about *Pride and Prejudice*: 'You say the book is indecent. You say I am
immodest. But Sir in the depiction of love, modesty is the fullness of truth;
and decency frankness; and so I must also be frank with you, and ask that
you remove my name from the title page in all future printings.'

8 Exactly where in Winchester Cathedral is Jane Austen buried?

9 How many printings did *Pride and Prejudice* have during Austen's lifetime?

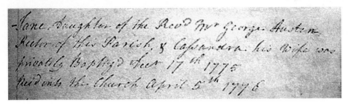

10 This is Jane's entry in the baptism register. Whose is the handwriting?

11 How many chapters of *Sanditon* did Jane complete before her death?

12 Who is this?

13 What is her relationship to Jane Austen?

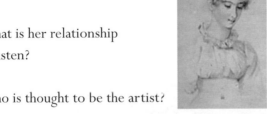

14 Who is thought to be the artist?

15 James, Jane's brother, had a first wife. What was her full name?

16 From whose diary is this extract taken?

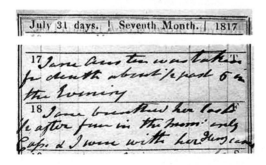

17 According to Sir Walter Scott '[Miss Austen] had a talent for describing …' what?

Locations and Buildings

1 Steventon is connected to Jane Austen but how?

2 Two major Austen novels are set in Bath. Which ones?

3 Lyme is a setting in *Emma*. True or false?

4 In *Mansfield Park*, where was Fanny Price's childhood home?
(a) Southampton   (b) Portsmouth   (c) Penzance

5 Where is the house in this photograph located?

6 Pemberley is to be found in *Pride and Prejudice*. True or false?

7 Where would you find a reference to Blaize Castle?

8 Northamptonshire is connected to one of the novels. Which one is it?

9 'As a house, Barton Cottage, though small, was comfortable and compact.' This description is from *Pride and Prejudice*. True or false?

10 In which novel would you find Kellynch Hall?

11 'A good sized entrance and two sitting-rooms made the length of the house.' This is a description of Chawton Cottage. True or false?

12 Name the novel in which you would find Netherfield Park.

13 Describe and locate the picture below.

14 'In a retired part of the County of Sussex there is a village called …' what?
(a) Evelyn   (b) Catherine   (c) Mansfield

15 In which novel would you find Hartfield?

1 Camden Place, Bath is the address. What is the novel?

2 'The bathing was so delightful this morning' wrote Jane in 1804 but where from?

3 In which of the novels would you find Beechen Cliff?

4 Identify this picture and explain its relationship to Jane.

5 Box Hill, Great Bookham and *Emma* are the clues. Can you link them?

6 '... as a cottage it was defective ... In comparison of Norland, it was poor and small indeed!' Where are these lines from?

7 Name the famous road in Bath that was completed in the year of Austen's birth.

8 Ramsgate is a location mentioned in two of the novels. Which ones are they?

9 'Are you pleased with Kent?' Who is speaking to whom?

10 Fullerton is the village in which the Morlands lived. In which county is it?

11 Identify this building. An extra point if you know who drew it.

12 'To an imagination which had hoped for the smallest divisions and the heaviest stone work, for painted glass, dirt, and cobwebs, the difference was very distressing.' To what do these lines refer?

13 What is this building and where is it?

14 Which spa town did Jane visit in 1816?

21

1 Identify this building and connect it to Jane.

2 Where did Mr and Mrs Thomas Knight II live?

3 In the summer of 1788, which places did Jane and Cassandra visit with their parents?

4 Jane Austen referred to it as the Great House. What was its name?

5 Locate this picture and connect it to the Austen family.

6 Where is *Sanditon* set?

7 'Everybody acquainted with Bath may remember the difficulties of crossing ...' which street?

8 'I do not call Tunbridge or Cheltenham the country'. Where is this line from?

9 Where is this and how is this building connected to the Austen family? Provide as exact an address as possible.

10 Explain the significance of Green Park Buildings.

11 'On her return to Crankhumdunberry (of which sweet village her father was Rector) ...' Where would you find this extract?

12 In which early work of Austen's would you find letters sent from Glenford, Bristol and Portman Square?

13 Where was Edward and George's school (Edward Austen's eldest sons)?

Locations and Buildings

1   What is the significance of San Domingo?

2   In August 1799, where was Mrs Leigh Perrot sent?

3   Name the location of this picture and its significance to Jane Austen.

4   When his wife died, where did James Austen send his daughter to live?

5   Explain the significance of Ashe Rectory.

6   Who was guillotined in Paris in 1794?

7   Explain the relevance of the name 'Petty Johns'.

9   According to the census of 1841, who exactly was living in Chawton Cottage?

10 In which of Jane's works would you find Trafalgar House?

11 What was the extent of the glebe at Steventon Rectory?

12 How is Cheesedown Farm connected to Jane Austen?

13 When was Steventon Rectory demolished and why?

14 Who lived at Hurstbourne Park and Hackwood Park and what is the significance of them to the Austen family?

15 Name and locate the building below.

16 'Beware of the unmeaning Luxuries of Bath and of the Stinking Fish of Southampton.' Where would you find these lines?

Courtships, Weddings and Marriages

1 In *Pride and Prejudice*, who does Elizabeth Bennet marry?

2 Match these heroines to their partners:

Emma	Fanny Price	Catherine Morland
Edmund Bertram	Mr Knightley	Henry Tilney

3 Mr Elton proposes marriage to Anne Elliot. True or false?

4 In *Sense and Sensibility*, who does Marianne Dashwood marry?

5 'They were gradually acquainted, and when acquainted, rapidly and deeply in love.' Where is this from?

6 'Almost as soon as I entered the house, I singled you out as the companion of my future life.' This is the caption for the C. E. Brock illustration shown to the right. Who are the two characters and what is the novel?

7 'Henry and Catherine were married, the bells rang, and everybody smiled.' Is this from:

(a) *Persuasion*   (b) *Emma*   (c) *Northanger Abbey*?

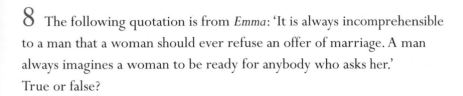

8 The following quotation is from *Emma*: 'It is always incomprehensible to a man that a woman should ever refuse an offer of marriage. A man always imagines a woman to be ready for anybody who asks her.' True or false?

9 'I never wish to act a more principal part at a Wedding than the superintending and directing the Dinner,' Is this from:
(a) *Emma*   (b) *Lesley Castle*   (c) *Sense and Sensibility*?

10 Name the actress in this picture.

11 'in short, Mr Harley soon found out that she was his Emma and recollected that he had married her a few weeks before he left England.' This is from *Emma*. True or false?

12 In *Sense and Sensibility*, which of the Dashwood sisters 'could never love by halves;'?

13 'She is not the first Girl who has gone to the East Indies for a Husband.' This is from *Catharine*. True or false?

14 'I cannot fix on the hour, or the spot, or the look, or the words, which laid the foundation. It is too long ago. I was in the middle before I knew that I had begun.' Who is speaking to whom?

Courtships, Weddings and Marriages

1 What is the relevance to Jane Austen of Harris Bigg-Wither?

2 'A clergyman like you must marry.' Where is this from and who is speaking to whom?

3 Their marriage takes place 'within a twelvemonth from the first day of their meeting'. Who are they?

4 'I would have everybody marry if they can do it properly: I do not like to have people throw themselves away: but everybody should marry as soon as they can do it to advantage.' Where are these lines from?

5 She 'gloried in being a sailor's wife'. Who is she?

6 In this illustration by C. E. Brock, who is showing her ring to the servants?

7 Where are the following lines from?
'You pierce my soul ...
I have loved none but you.'

8 At the end of *Pride and Prejudice*, Mr Bennet says 'I admire all my three sons-in-law highly,' but who are they? An extra point if you know who 'perhaps, is my favourite'.

9 According to Austen, marriage is 'a great …' what?

10 Mr Collins gives three reasons why he should marry.
Name as many of them as you can.

11 The following is from *Emma*. 'the happiness of the married cousins must appear as secure as earthly happiness can be.'
True or false?

12 Supply the three missing words: 'A lady's imagination is very — ;
it jumps from — to love, from love to — in a moment.'
An extra point if you can name the book.

13 'He is the most horrible flirt that can be imagined.' Who is he?

14 Who was 'very deeply mortified by Darcy's marriage'?

15 The following is taken from an early work of Austen's but what is it? 'Sophia and I experienced the Satisfaction of seeing them depart for Gretna-Green, which they chose for the celebration of their Nuptials.'

Courtships, Weddings and Marriages

1 What is the relationship between the Austen family and the Revd Tom Fowle?

2 Who 'married, in the common phrase, to disoblige her family'?

3 The following is from *The History of England* but which King is Austen referring to? 'He married Anne of Denmark and had several children.'

4 Who did Martha Lloyd marry?

5 'It was a very proper wedding. The bride was elegantly dressed;' but the two bridesmaids were what?

6 As a postscript to his letter at the end of *Persuasion*, what does Frederick Wentworth say 'will be enough to decide whether I enter your father's house this evening, or never'?

7 'I have disconcerted him already by my calm reserve.' Where would you find this?

8 'He instantly made her an offer of his hand and his heart, which she graciously condescended to accept,' This is from *Volume the Third* but which work?

9 'Equally formed for domestic life, and attached to country pleasures, their home was the home of affection and comfort;' Identify them.

10 'the wedding clothes were brought and nothing remained to be settled but the naming of the day.' Where is this from?

11 The following is from *Mansfield Park* – complete the missing words. 'Mr and Mrs Norris began their career of conjugal felicity with very little less than —'

12 Who had 'reached an age highly suitable for dancing, and not very ineligible for being supposed to have a lover'?

13 Name the person alluded to in the following: 'she felt her approach to the years of danger, and would have rejoiced to be certain of being properly solicited by baronet-blood within the next twelvemonth or two.'

14 In a letter to Cassandra, Jane says, 'We have heard nothing fresh from Anna.' To what does this refer?

15 'Single Women have a dreadful propensity for being poor – which is one very strong argument in favour of Matrimony,'. Who is speaking to whom?

Courtships, Weddings and Marriages

1 E. H. are her initials. She was related to Jane but what was the nationality of her husband?

2 The place is Bermuda, the date is 19 May 1807. Whose wedding is this?

3 'I would rather be a teacher at a school (and I can think of nothing worse) than marry a man I did not like.' Name the work from which these lines are taken.

4 Alethea Bigg's sister, Catherine, was married to the Rector of Streatham. What was his name?

5 Jane writes to Fanny Knight: 'you like him well enough to marry, but not well enough to wait.' Who is he?

6 This picture is of a Regency wedding dress – whose is it?

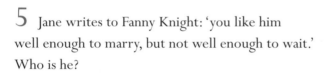

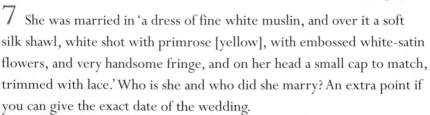

7 She was married in 'a dress of fine white muslin, and over it a soft silk shawl, white shot with primrose [yellow], with embossed white-satin flowers, and very handsome fringe, and on her head a small cap to match, trimmed with lace.' Who is she and who did she marry? An extra point if you can give the exact date of the wedding.

8 Where would you find the letter 'From a Young Lady very much in love'?

9 Firstly, identify and locate this building and explain its significance to Regency weddings. A bonus point if you know the architect. Secondly, Mary Anne Lewis and Harriet Westbrook were both married here. Can you identify their husbands?
(A clue – one was an English poet, the other a politician and future Prime Minister).

10 The clues are: Eleanor Jackson, 1820 and a second marriage. Who is the person?

11 The following is from *Mansfield Park*. Can you supply the missing words? 'her mother stood with salts in her hand, expecting to be —; her aunt tried — —;'

12 In *Persuasion*, what does Anne claim as 'All the privilege ... for my own sex'?

13 Complete the missing words taken from a letter to Fanny Knight: 'Anything is to be — or — rather than marrying — —'

14 Taken from *A Collection of Letters*, what is the 'only kind of love I would give a farthing for'?

Identify the Novel

1 'It is a truth universally acknowledged, that a single man in possession of a good fortune, must be in want of a wife.' Which novel opens with these lines?

2 Of the six major novels, only two have one-word titles. Which ones are they?

3 Colonel Brandon is a character from *Northanger Abbey*. True or false?

4 The caption to this illustration is 'While Fanny cut the roses.' From this, identify the novel.

5 *Love and Freindship* is found in *Volume the Second*. True or false?

6 Match these characters to the novels in which they are found:

Mr Collins   Anne Elliot   Elinor Dashwood

Sense and Sensibility   *Pride and Prejudice*   *Persuasion*

7 *Sanditon* is named after a place, as are two of the major novels. Which are they?

8 'A woman should never be trusted with money.' This is from *Emma*. True or false?

9 The character in this illustration by Hugh Thomson is Mrs Ferrars. Identify the novel in which you would find her.

10 Identify the novels which contain the following characters:
(a) Mary Bennet (b) Camilla (c) Catherine Morland

11 'Every neighbourhood should have a great lady.'
Where is this line from?
(a) *Catharine* (b) *Pride and Prejudice* (c) *Sanditon*

12 Sophy, Georgiana and Mary Stanhope are found in *The Three Sisters*. True or false?

13 Name the novels in which you would find these characters:
(a) Colonel Campbell (b) General Tilney (c) Captain Harville

Identify the Novel

1 Which was the first of Jane Austen's novels to be published?

2 Identify this early work from the illustration below.

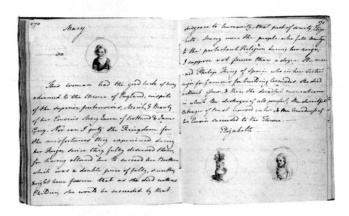

3 Two novels were published posthumously. Name them.

4 'I should like to know who is the author, for it is much too clever to have been written by a woman.' Identify the 'it'.

5 One of the novels is dedicated to the Prince Regent. Which is it?

6 Can you name the novel this illustration appears in?

7 In which book would you find a production called *Lovers' Vows*?

8 Which work from *Volume the Second* is described as 'a novel in a series of letters'?

9 Published fourteen years after its earliest version had been written – what is it?

10 Begun in August 1815, this novel took almost exactly a year to write. Name it.

11 Identify the novel whose heroine is described as being 'spoiled by being the cleverest of her family. At ten years old, she had the misfortune of being able to answer questions that puzzled her sister at seventeen.'

12 'By the author of "Sense and Sensibility"'.
This is a title page from one of the novels; which one is it?

13 'an unfinished Novel in Letters', the first letter being from Miss Margaret Lesley to Miss Charlotte Lutterell. What is it?

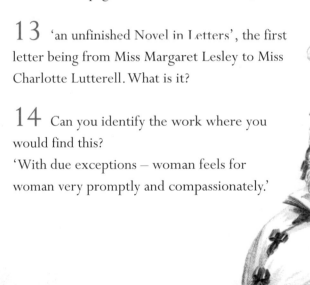

14 Can you identify the work where you would find this?
'With due exceptions – woman feels for woman very promptly and compassionately.'

Identify the Novel

1 'lop't and crop't' – Jane's own words, but which two novels are they linked to?

2 The clues are Emma, her sister and this exchange: 'I think I could like any good humoured man with a comfortable income.' What is the work?

3 'Good apple pies are a considerable part of our domestic happiness.' Identify the piece of writing from which this is taken.

4 Where would you find *The Adventures of Mr Harley*?

5 John Murray is connected to which novels and why?

6 'the Bower' is its subtitle. What is it?

7 Which drama is dedicated to James Austen?

8 'I shall be able to manage the Sir-loin myself; my Mother will eat the Soup, and You and the Doctor must finish the rest. Here I was interrupted, by seeing my poor Sister fall down, to appearance Lifeless, upon one of the Chests, where we keep our Table linen.' Where would you find these lines?

9 Which work's opening lines tell us that the heroine has lost her parents when she was very young?

10 One of the works in *Volume the First* is dedicated to Miss Cooper. Which one is it?

11 Which early work is 'a novel in twelve Chapters'?

12 In a dedication to Martha Lloyd, Jane writes 'for your late generosity to me in finishing my muslin Cloak.' Can you identify the work?

13 Which of Austen's early works includes *The Visit* and *The Mystery*?

Identify the Novel

1 Jane sold one of her novels for £10 and made a stipulation about its publication. Identify both the novel and the stipulation.

2 Which accomplishments (there are six) will gain a woman 'some applause' but will not add what to 'her list'? Identify the work.

3 Where would you find the characters called Popgun, Strephon and Chloe?

4 Which work is dedicated to Madame La Comtesse de Feuillide?

5 'I can no more forget it, than a mother can forget her suckling child.' So wrote Jane in a letter to Cassandra but what is 'it'?

6 J. M. and 2,000 are the clues. What is the answer?

7 In an unfinished comedy by Austen, you will find Daphne, Fanny Elliott and Mrs Humbug. What is it called?

8 The Military Library, Whitehall is the clue. From this, can you make a connection to three of Austen's novels?

9 Which novel, although never reviewed, sold well enough to make Jane £350?

10 In which work would you find Mr Webb and Mr Gower?

11 'The accident happened just beyond the only gentleman's house near the lane a house which their driver, on being first required to take that direction, had conceived to be necessarily their object and had with most unwilling looks been constrained to pass by.'
Where would you find this extract?

12 £110 is the clue. What is the answer?

13 What is the connection between this magazine and one of Jane's novels?

THE
NEW MONTHLY MAGAZINE.

No. 25.] FEBRUARY 1, 1816. [Vol. V.

MONTHLY MAGAZINES have opened a way for every kind of inquiry and information. The intelligence and discussion contained in them are very extensive and various; and they have been the means of diffusing a general habit of reading through the nation, which in a certain degree both enlarged the public understanding. HERE, too, are preserved a multitude of useful hints, observations, and facts, which otherwise might never have appeared.—Dr. Kippis.

Every Art is improved by the emulation of Competitors.—Dr. Johnson.

66 New Publications, with Critical Remarks. [Feb. 1,

14 'somewhere about February 1811'.
What is the significance of these words?

Who or What is This?

1 Who is this?

2 Who was 'too diffident to do justice to himself;'?
(a) Mr Darcy   (b) Mr Knightley   (c) Mr Ferrars?

3 Name two characters in the novels who are called Jane.

4 'Had she been tall, full formed, and fair, it might have been more of a trial.' This refers to Emma – true or false?

5 The three pictures below are of Regency dresses. Exactly when would each of them be worn?

(a)   (b)   (c)

6 'She was a woman of mean understanding, little information, and uncertain temper.' Who is she?

7 One of Jane's brothers was made a Lieutenant at the age of seventeen. Which one was it?

8 Which King was on the throne during Jane's lifetime?

9 Whose father is called Sir Walter?

10 Connect the person in the picture below to Jane Austen. Extra points if you can name her parents.

Who or What is This?

11 Henry and Mary are brother and sister, and are found in *Mansfield Park*. What is their surname?

12 Who is 'so odd a mixture of quick parts, sarcastic humour, reserve and caprice'?

13 Identify these two characters from the following quotes:
(a) 'She was small of her age, with no glow of complexion, nor any other striking beauty;'
(b) 'her sorrows, her joys, could have no moderation.'

14 The initials of the person in the picture below are M. L. and she was a friend of Jane's. Who is she?

15 'They were a remarkably fine family, the sons very well-looking, the daughters decidedly handsome, and all of them well grown and forward of their age.' Identify both the family and the book.

Who or What is This?

1 What is this?

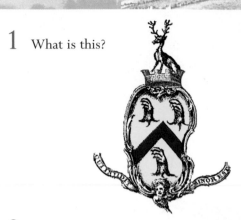

2 In 1870 who published *A Memoir of Jane Austen*?

3 Which heroine was born on 9 August 1787?

4 Explain the relationship between the following families and the Austens: the Chutes, the Heathcotes and the Bramstons.

5 The following is from *Northanger Abbey* – complete the quotation and identify the character. 'She had a most harmless delight in being — '

6 F. B. are the initials of someone connected to Austen. Can you identify her?

7 Who says 'My sister has often trusted me in the choice of a gown'?
(a) Mr Tilney   (b) Captain Wentworth   (c) Mr Collins

8 In the picture below, name both subject and painter and connect it to Jane Austen.

9 'they were still near neighbours and intimate friends; and one remained a widower, the other a widow.' Who are they?

10 Who, in the first chapter of the book in which she appears, is described as 'a good-humoured, well-disposed girl;'?

11 This picture is of George Crabbe. Can you explain his significance to Jane Austen?

12 Can you name one of Austen's favourite writers whose surname begins with 'J'?

13 'Do you understand muslins, sir?' This is from *Northanger Abbey*, but can you name the people in this conversation?

14 These portraits are of three of Jane's brothers. Can you identify them?

(a)

(b)

(c)

15 Austen used her sister-in-laws' Christian names for some of her characters. Name as many as you can.

Who or What is This?

1 Can you connect Jane Austen to the person in this picture?

2 The clues are 10.20 a.m. and 19 January 1805. What is the answer?

3 Who is Dordy and what is his relationship to Jane?

4 'Now I will prepare for Mr Lushington.' Who is he and where is this reference to him found?

5 Identify both the painter and the subject in this picture. Extra points if you can date the picture and name the book in which you would find it.

6 'He's a rogue of course, but a civil one.' Who is Austen describing?

7 An earlier question referred to Mrs Leigh Perrot. How is she connected to Jane and why was she arrested and imprisoned?

8 In a letter to Cassandra, Jane writes: 'Remember that Aunt Cassandras are quite as scarce as Miss Beverleys.' Explain the reference to 'Miss Beverleys'.

9 Explain the connection between Mrs Ashton Dennis and a letter to Crosby in April 1809.

10 Identify the person in this picture, giving his full name and title and connect him to Jane.

11 Identify the king described by Austen as follows in *The History of England*: 'This unfortunate Prince lived so little a while that no body had time to draw his picture.'

12 This is a picture of Samuel Richardson. What is his connection to one of Jane's early works?

13 Connect this coat of arms to Jane Austen.

Who or What is This?

1 The pictures below are of people who lived, or events that occurred, during Austen's lifetime. Identify them as fully as you can.

(a)

(b)

(c)

2 Make the connection between Emily St Aubert and Jane Austen.

3 Mrs Knight considered a certain rector of Chawton to be an eligible husband for Jane. Who was he?

4 On whose death did Jane write her only known serious poem?

5 The clues are March 1816 and the initials H. A. What is the answer?

6 Name the person who reviewed *Emma* in the *Edinburgh Review*.

7 *Which is the Heroine?* was a second novel but who wrote it?

8 Identify the person in the picture below and connect him to Austen.

9 J. M. and W. G. are the initials. Can you identify and connect them?

10 'downright nonsense' was an opinion of *Sense and Sensibility* and *Pride and Prejudice* – whose opinion was it?

11 Name the person who regarded *Love and Freindship* as 'the most amusing and incisive of all eighteenth-century attacks upon sentimental fiction'.

12 Identify these women:
(a) In 1798, when driving herself in a one-horse chaise, she was involved in an accident and died;
(b) In 1804 she died after falling from a horse.

13 Which character lived in Bath and had never seen London?

Pride and Prejudice

1 Lydia Bennet is the heroine of *Pride and Prejudice*. True or false?

2 How many daughters does Mrs Bennet have?
(a) four   (b) five   (c) six

3 Name as many of them as you can.

4 Which family is particularly friendly with the Bennets?

5 Who is this and which role did he play?

6 What is the relationship between Mr Darcy and Mr Bingley?

7 'I am going to Greta Green.' Who writes this?

8 How old is Elizabeth Bennet?
(a) 19   (b) 27   (c) 20

9 There have been two BBC adaptations of *Pride and Prejudice* between 1980 and 1995. True or false?

10 Link the picture below to *Pride and Prejudice*.

11 What is Darcy's first name?

12 'I am not afraid; for though I *am* the youngest, I'm the tallest.' Identify this character.

13 'a tall, large woman, with strongly-marked features, which might once have been handsome.' Who is she?

14 'He was a tall, heavy looking young man of five and twenty. His air was grave and stately, and his manners were very formal.' Who is he?

Pride and Prejudice

1 Identify this character: 'A good humoured girl ... [who] had nothing to say that could be worth hearing.'

2 'One came from her books, and the other from her toilette.' Name the two Bennet sisters described here.

3 Lydia writes a letter, telling of her intentions to marry Mr Wickham. Who is it written to?

4 In this illustration by H. M. Brock, who is the elderly lady standing closest to the portraits?

5 As regards travelling, what does Lady Catherine consider to be 'highly improper'?

6 At the end of *Pride and Prejudice*, who is 'the only daughter who remained at home'?

7 When was the first stage adaptation of *Pride and Prejudice*?

8 'the work is rather too light, and bright, and sparkling; it wants shade …' Who said this of *Pride and Prejudice*?

9 How are Deborah Moggach and Fay Weldon connected to *Pride and Prejudice*?

10 'Are the shades of Pemberley to be thus polluted?' Who is speaking?

11 Identify the two male characters in this Hugh Thomson illustration.

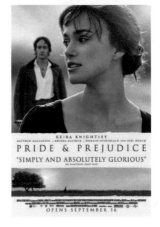

12 This is Keira Knightley in the role of Lizzie Bennet but in this film adaptation who played the following roles:
(a) Mrs Bennet
(b) Lady Catherine de Burgh?

13 Name the two stars in the 1940 screen adaptation of *Pride and Prejudice*.

14 Mr Bingley has a well-to-do brother-in-law; what is his name?

Pride and Prejudice

1 *Pride and Prejudice* was published at whose expense?

2 What was the profession of Mrs Bennet's father and where had he worked?

3 Look at the picture below.
Who wrote the screenplay for this adaptation?

4 How much money had Mrs Bennet been left by her father?

5 Why was the title of *First Impressions* altered to *Pride and Prejudice*?

6 'buy it immediately' for it 'was one of the cleverest things' he had ever read. Who said this of *Pride and Prejudice*?

7 In which year did Jane write *First Impressions*?

8 'It was a journey of only twenty-four miles, and they began it so early as to be in Gracechurch-street by noon.' Who are they?

9 Who, in 1940, wrote a screenplay of the novel for MGM?

10 'I have got my own darling Child from London.'
Explain the significance of this to *Pride and Prejudice*.

11 In one film version of the novel, Mr Collins is given a new profession. What is it?

12 In the 1952 TV version, name the actress who played opposite Peter Cushing.

13 Grosvenor Street and Gracechurch Street are the addresses but who lives there?

Pride and Prejudice

1 'The disagreement subsisting between yourself and my late honoured father, always gave me much uneasiness.' So writes Mr Collins to Mr Bennet, but what is the exact address given at the top of the letter?

2 A. A. M. are his initials. Who is he and what is his connection to *Pride and Prejudice*?

3 How is *Cecilia* by Fanny Burney connected to *Pride and Prejudice*?

4 Talking to her family about the characters she created after the novels were finished, who does Jane say Kitty Bennet married?

5 'a very superior work … the most probable fiction I have ever read.' Who said this in a letter to her mother?

6 When was the third edition of *Pride and Prejudice* published?

7 'The greatest blunder in the Printing that I have met with …' This is taken from a letter by Austen to Cassandra. Specify exactly what the blunder is?

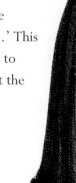

8 Below is a title page
of a 1907 edition with the
publisher's name obscured.
Who published it in London
and who in New York?

9 Approximately how many copies of the first edition were printed?

10 When did the first edition of *Pride and Prejudice* sell out?
Give the month and year.

11 Who wrote the lyrics to the Broadway musical *First Impressions*?
An extra point if you know who wrote the music.

12 H. G. are her initials, and she appeared in the Broadway version.
Who is she and which part did she play?

13 What is the significance of the Derbyshire Militia to *First Impressions*?

14 Give the publication day and year of *Pride and Prejudice*.

Sense and Sensibility

1 How many daughters are there in the Dashwood family?

2 Elinor Dashwood is aged nineteen. True or false?

3 In which county is this novel set?

4 How do Marianne and Willoughby meet?

5 What is the relationship between Mrs Jennings and Lady Middleton?

6 Match these names correctly:
  Edward   Lucy   Fanny
  Steele   Dashwood   Ferrars

7 Name the actress and the role she played.

8 What is Ang Lee's connection to this adaptation?

9 Henry Dashwood had children by a former marriage; how many did he have?

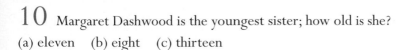

10 Margaret Dashwood is the youngest sister; how old is she?
(a) eleven   (b) eight   (c) thirteen

11 He is 'uncommonly handsome'. Who is he?
(a) Henry Dashwood   (b) Willoughby   (c) Colonel Brandon

12 Both Marianne and Margaret consider Colonel Brandon to be an elderly bachelor; approximately how old is he?

13 'She had an excellent heart; her disposition was excellent; and her feelings were strong.' Who is she?

14 Identify the two characters in this C. E. Brock illustration.

Sense and Sensibility

1 When the novel opens, in which county has the Dashwood family been living?

2 Identify these people from their initials:
(a) R. F.   (b) J. D.   (c) J. M.

3 In this illustration, who are the two characters?

4 'I never saw a young woman so desperately in love in my life!' Who is speaking about whom?

5 'He hunted and shot; she humoured her children; and these were their only resources.' Who are they?

6 A substantial part of the novel is set in which city?

7 Mrs Dashwood and her daughters manage to live on an annual income of what?

8 Name the character who idled away the mornings at billiards.

9   What should he have been doing instead?

10   Identify the actors in this picture and the characters they play.

11   How much is Edward Ferrars' annual stipend?

12   In which county does Willoughby have an estate?

13   Whose marriage 'divided her as little from her family as could well be contrived'?

14   At the end of the novel, Mrs Dashwood remains at the cottage without moving where?

15   Name the actor and the character he plays.

Sense and Sensibility

1 When Elinor and Marianne travel to London with Mrs Jennings, how long is their journey?

2 Say as precisely as possible when this journey takes place.

3 How is Willoughby first described? What type of dog does he have with him and how many?

4 Six adjectives are used to introduce Mrs Jennings. Name as many of them as you can.

5 'At seventeen she was lost to me forever.' Identify the characters and explain the situation.

6 Identify this actress, say which part she played and date the adaptation.

7 In the Hugh Thomson illustration below, who is the character with the horse?

8 The clues are £1,000 per year and £10,000. Explain.

9 Who has rooms in Pall Mall?

10 Elinor has two qualities that allow her to be 'the counselor of her mother'. What are they?

11 When was this adaptation released and who directed it?

12 Margaret Dashwood is not a major character in the novel. However, she is involved in two incidents.
What are they?

1 'It must be nonsense with a title like that.' Name the person who said this about *Sense and Sensibility* when it was first published.

2 Connect this picture to an adaptation of *Sense and Sensibility*, answering the following:
(a) What is its English title?   (b) Who directed it?
(c) What is the language of the film?

3 According to Marianne, what is the only thing that kept Edward from Harley Street?

4 Jane's niece, Anna, the Alton Circulating Library and the first volume of *Sense and Sensibility* are the clues. Can you connect them?

5 This is the title page of an illustrated edition that appeared in 1908. It was published as part of a series. What was the series called?

6 On what date exactly was *Sense and Sensibility* published?

7 How much did it cost and how many volumes were in the first edition?

8 'It is a clever novel … and, though it ends stupidly, I was much amused by it.' Name the person who said this about *Sense and Sensibility*.

9 Who did she say it to?

10 Where in London do the following people live:
(a) The John Dashwoods (b) Sir John Middleton (c) Mrs Jennings

11 St James's Street is the address – who lives there?

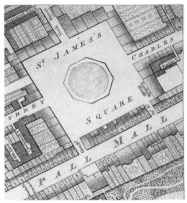

12 Where do the Steeles live?

13 What is the significance of the characters in questions 10–12 living where they do?

14 At the end of the novel, Marianne and Elinor are living near to one another but despite this they could live 'without — between themselves or producing — between — —'. Supply the missing words.

1 What is Emma's second name?

2 Abbey Mill Farm is the home for which family?

3 Emma has a brother. True or false?

4 'he was gone off to London, merely to have his hair cut.' Who is he?

5 What is Mrs Goddard's profession?

6 Match these names correctly:

| Jane | Harriet | Frank |
| Smith | Churchill | Fairfax |

7 At the beginning of *Emma*, how old is Emma?

8 Mr Elton lives at Randalls. True or false?

9 What is Mr Knightley's first name?

10 Whose 'frequent visits were one of the comforts of Mr Woodhouse's life'?
(a) Isabella   (b) Mr Perry   (c) Emma

11 Emma wants to matchmake but who are the two people involved?

12 'a young man living alone without liking it.' Who is he?

13 Who is Mr Knightley's brother married to?

14 What is the name of this actress who appeared in the title role of the 1996 film adaptation?

15 At the beginning of *Emma* there is a wedding; whose is it?

1 Which three adjectives are used to describe Emma in the opening lines of the novel?

2 What colour are Emma's eyes?

3 Approximately how much older than Emma is Mr Knightley?

4 'Mr Knightley might quarrel with her, but Emma could not quarrel with …' who?

5 Name the place that is described as 'an inconsiderable house … where a pair of post-horses were kept.'

6 Miss Hawkins' first name is related to a month; which one is it?

7 Who is the clergyman who officiates at Harriet's wedding?

8 Bella, George, Henry and John – who are they?

9 According to Mr Knightley, who was the only person able to cope with Emma?

10 Emma refers to certain people as 'yeomanry'. What does she feel about them?

11 What is the relationship between Frank Churchill and Jane Fairfax?

12 'I think her the very worst sort of companion that Emma could possibly have.' Who is speaking about whom?

13 Which two characters are associated with Weymouth?

14 Look at the picture below. Who played Emma in this adaptation and who was Mr Knightley?

15 This adaptation came out in 1995. True or false?

16 What is Mr Perry's profession?

1 At the end of *Emma*, where is Jane Fairfax living?

2 Date this edition of Emma, and give the name of the illustrator. This information has been obscured in the version below.

3 The youngest of two daughters, her father is a Bristol merchant and she had spent part of every winter in Bath – who is she?

4 Identify the two characters in this picture.

5 Mrs Bates is 'almost past everything', except two things. What are they?

6 Emma paints Harriet Smith's portrait; do you know the medium in which it is painted? An extra point if you can add any more information.

7 Where does Emma intend to hang this picture?

8 Explain the link between Mrs Smallridge and Jane Fairfax.

9 'I wish our opinions were the same.'
Mr Knightley is speaking to Emma; what is the subject?

10 Mr Woodhouse is very fussy about his food.
Whose boiled eggs does he particularly recommend to Miss Bates?

11 Miss Bates is extremely popular and yet she is lacking four qualities. What are they?

12 Name the character who is 'first seen at church'.

13 Harriet shows Emma a parcel marked, 'Most precious treasures.'
When the parcel is unwrapped, what type of box is revealed?
Be as precise as you can.

14 September and October are the months of the weddings;
whose are they?

15 Explain the association between the Perry children and Mrs Weston's wedding cake.

16 What are the final six words of *Emma*?

Emma

1   Complete this riddle:
Kitty, a fair but frozen maid,
Kindled a flame I yet deplore.

2   Who is this riddle attributed to?

3   Why does Austen say that 'a young person, who either marries or dies, is sure of being kindly spoken of.'?

4   Name the actress who played *Emma* in this adaptation and date it.

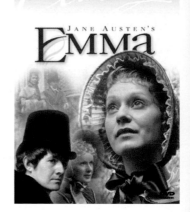

5   In an earlier question relating to Mrs Bates, there is a reference to quadrille. What is quadrille?

6   The clues are: christened, Catherine, grandmother. What is the answer?

7   Name the three people who Mrs Goddard invites to supper, their professions and what they are given to eat. An extra point if you know who has provided the food.

8   What is the significance of the *Vicar of Wakefield*, *Romance of the Forest* and *Children of the Abbey*?

9 What are Mrs Elton's criticisms of Emma's wedding?

10 Early in the novel, Harriet talks to Emma about Abbey Mill Farm and the Martin family.
(a) Which room does she mention specifically and how many of these rooms are there?
(b) How long has the maid been with them?
(c) How many cows do they have and which two breeds are mentioned?

11 Twenty-four years old, 8 June and 23 June.
Can you link these clues?

12 Frank Churchill is keen to organize a ball. Initial discussion involves five couples being invited. How many of the women can you name?

13 When Mr and Mrs Elton initially visit Hartfield, what is the first topic of conversation between Emma and Augusta?

14 Who is Mr Suckling?

15 Name the actor who played Mr Knightley in this adaptation and the director.

EMMA [U]

JANE AUSTEN

BBC TV's delightful adaptation of Jane Austen's witty, observant and romantic masterpiece

1 'She had a thin awkward figure, a sallow skin without colour, dark lank hair, and strong features.' Who is she?

2 The Morlands are a large family; how many children are there exactly?
(a) ten   (b) seven   (c) five

3 Identify the character in this picture.

4 How do Mrs Thorpe and Mrs Allen know each other? Are they:
(a) cousins   (b) sisters-in-law   (c) school friends?

5 Match these names correctly:
    Henry   John   James
    Morland   Thorpe   Tilney

6 If a woman has 'the misfortune of knowing anything', should she reveal or conceal it?

7 *Northanger Abbey* was first known by a woman's name. What was it?

8 'Catherine's disposition was not naturally ... what?
(a) industrious (b) sedentary

9 Identify the two characters
in this drawing.

"Always arm-in-arm when they walked"
Chap X

10 Who is older, Catherine or Isabella? An extra point if you know by
how many years.

11 'a brown skin, with dark eyes, and rather dark hair.' Who is he?

12 Catherine's father is called Richard. True or false?

13 What is his profession?

14 Isabella had 'a good figure, a pretty face, and a very agreeable
countenance'. True or false?

1 'Her love of dirt gave way to an inclination for finery.' This describes Catherine Morland; how old is she at this point?

2 'a widow, and not a very rich one.' Who is she?

3 Look at the picture below and identify the elderly couple.

4 Why is Mr Allen told to go to Bath?

5 'You will allow that in both man has the advantage of choice, woman only the power of refusal.'
What are the two situations Henry Tilney is referring to?

6 What is the significance of Mrs Radcliffe?

7 'Friendship is certainly the finest balm for ...' what?

8 The actress is Catherine Walker in the BBC 2007 adaptation; what part is she playing?

9 From between which ages is Catherine 'in training for a heroine'?

10 When Catherine and the Allens first arrive in Bath, where are their lodgings?

11 'Lord help me! You women are always thinking of men's being in liquor.' Who is speaking?

12 Who says: 'I consider a country-dance as an emblem of marriage'?

13 In this novel, how much time is actually spent at Northanger Abbey?

14 How far is Woodston from Northanger Abbey?

Northanger Abbey

1 When Mrs Thorpe discusses her children with Mrs Allen early on in the novel, what do we learn about John, Edward and William?

2 How much did John Thorpe pay for his curricle?

3 Who changed Jane's original title of the book to *Northanger Abbey* and when

4 According to Henry Tilney, what is the name of 'the ancient housekeeper'?

'Can you stand such a ceremony as this!'

5 In this novel, approximately how many weeks are spent in Bath and how much time is spent at Fullerton?

6 Complete the missing words: 'In spite of — and the dressmaker, however, the party from — Street reached the — — in very good time.'

7 'it did not appear to her that life could supply any greater felicity.' To what does this line refer?

8 When was the first version of *Northanger Abbey* written?

9 Who played Mrs Allen in this adaptation?

10 In the first chapter, four influential writers who made an impression on Catherine are quoted. Name as many of them as you can.

11 At the end of *Northanger Abbey*, 'the tendency of this work' is said to be one of two things. What are they?

12 In an early conversation between Isabella and Catherine, Isabella refers to seven books recommended to her by a friend. Name as many of them as you can.

13 Identify the friend who is referred to in the preceding question.

14 In Chapter Two, which two adjectives are used to describe the mind of a seventeen-year-old girl?

15 According to John Thorpe, what would be a 'famous good thing for us all'?

1 In the opening pages of this novel, what does Austen say that Catherine has learned from Pope?

2 From the same place in the novel, complete these lines and identify their author:

> '*Many a flower is born to blush unseen,*
> *And ...*'

3 At their first meeting, Henry and Catherine are interrupted by Mrs Allen. What does she ask Catherine to do?

4 In the same conversation, she refers to the price of material. How much is it per yard?

5 When Isabella asks Catherine whether she likes dark or fair haired men best, what does Catherine reply?
There are some six points in her answer.

6 Identify the two characters in the picture and see if you can supply the caption – or as close to it as you can get.

7 Catherine Morland is said to lie awake for 'ten minutes on Wednesday night debating ...' what?

8 What is the meaning of 'tamboured'?

9 Early on in *Northanger Abbey*, Catherine, in a conversation with Isabella, mentions a book that her mother reads.
What is the book?

10 What is Isabella's response to this book?
Your answer should contain two points.

11 The clues are Sam Fletcher and a house in Leicestershire.
What is the answer?

12 Forty guineas is the price of a horse but whose is it?

13 Complete the quotation: 'Frederick will not be the first man who has ...'.

14 When Catherine visits Woodston, who does she go with and what does she travel in? An extra point if you know what time they set off.

15 Link these lines to *Northanger Abbey*: 'like Patience on a monument / Smiling at Grief.'

Mansfield Park

1 *Mansfield Park* was written by Jane Austen when she was thirty-six. True or false?

2 What is the relationship between Mrs Norris and Frances Ward?

3 When Fanny first arrives in Northampton, who meets her?
(a) Mrs Norris   (b) Lady Bertram   (c) Edmund

4 At what age does Fanny come to live with the Bertrams?
(a) eleven   (b) ten   (c) seven

5 With whom does Mr Yates elope?

6 'Complete in his lieutenant's uniform.'
This is the caption for this C. E. Brock
illustration. Who is the man?

7 Match the following names correctly:

Fanny   Mary   Edmund

Bertram   Price   Crawford

8 Fanny is given an animal by the Bertrams; what is it?

9 This adaptation of *Mansfield Park* was released in 1999. True or false?

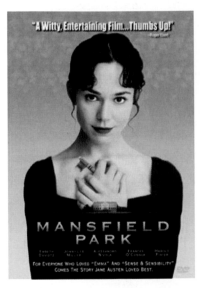

10 How many children are there in the Bertram family?

11 Jane Austen's mother preferred *Mansfield Park* to *Pride and Prejudice*. True or false?

12 If Austen's heroines are divided into those who are extrovert and those who are introvert, what would Fanny Price be?

13 Lady Bertram has a dog; what is its exact breed?

1 'he was plain, to be sure, but then he had so much countenance, and his teeth were so good, and he was so well made, that one soon forgot he was plain …' Who is he?

2 As regards her daughters, Lady Bertram paid not the smallest attention to what?

3 Name all of the Bertram children.

4 In this illustration, identify the male character.

5 'He might have made her childhood happier …' Who is he?

6 In which country is Sir Thomas Bertram's overseas estate?

7 'My plan is to make — in love with me.' Who is speaking about whom?

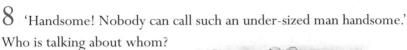

8 'Handsome! Nobody can call such an under-sized man handsome.'
Who is talking about whom?

9 Identify the two characters
in this illustration.

*Indulged with his
favourite instrument*

10 Who elopes with Maria Rushworth?

11 Who said that *Mansfield Park* had more sense in it than
Pride and Prejudice?

12 Over what period of time does the action in *Mansfield Park* take
place?
(a) a period of years less than ten
(b) less than five
(c) less than twenty

13 In the play *Lovers' Vows*, who takes the part of Count Cassel?

14 Which part is Mary Crawford given?

1 When Mr Norris dies, Mrs Norris moves first to one place and then to another. Where exactly does she go?

2 The Bertram girls have a tutor; what is her name?

3 Identify as many of the characters as you can in this C. E. Brock illustration.

4 Name the person who, at the end of the novel, becomes the 'stationary niece'.

5 It was once the schoolroom and is now Fanny's. What is it known as?

6 William is given some money by Lady Bertram. How much?

7 According to Mary Crawford, name the mother who is desperate for Henry to marry her daughter and what is the daughter called?

8 Where exactly does Mrs Norris suggest that Lady Bertram will put Fanny when she comes to Mansfield Park?

9 What is the date of this title page?

10 William gives Fanny a cross. What is it made of and where does it come from?

11 According to Mr Rushworth, how tall is Henry Crawford?

12 Supply the missing word: 'If you could discover whether Northamptonshire is a country of ...'

13 'An engaged woman' is always more what than a disengaged one?

14 Fanny's home is described as 'the abode of — — —'.
Supply as many as you can of the three missing words.

REQUIRING RESEARCH   *Mansfield Park*

1 The following is from a letter Jane wrote to Cassandra – who exactly is 'he' and 'them'? 'It is the most sensible novel he ever read, and the manner in which I treat the clergy delights them very much.'

2 Who is this and what is his connection to *Mansfield Park*?

3 At the end of the novel, what becomes particularly dear to Fanny?

4 Identify the actress in this 1983 BBC adaptation.

5 Look at this illustration and supply the caption. It need not be word-perfect but should be as close to the spirit of the original as possible.

6 Name the person who said of *Mansfield Park* that it was 'so evidently written by a gentlewoman'.

7 In Fanny's room, there are three 'transparencies'. Describe their settings.

8 According to Mary Crawford, what are her 'standards of perfection'?

9 When Edmund and Fanny are looking at the night sky, which two constellations do they identify?

10 'Happy Julia! Unhappy Maria!' Explain why this should be.

11 *Mansfield Park* contains a reference to a fable by Sterne. What is the creature in the fable?

12 In which of Sterne's works would you find it?

13 Anhalt and the Butler are the clues. How are they connected to two of the characters in the novel?

Persuasion

1 How many sisters does Anne Elliot have?

2 How old was Austen when she wrote *Persuasion*?
(a) 19   (b) 29   (c) 40

3 In which county is Kellynch Hall?
(a) Somerset   (b) Herefordshire   (c) Shropshire

4 The novel has two main urban locations. Name them.

5 Identify the character in this illustration by C. E. Brock.

Few women could think more of their personal appearance than he did.

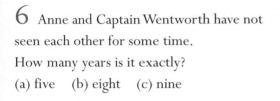

6 Anne and Captain Wentworth have not seen each other for some time. How many years is it exactly?
(a) five   (b) eight   (c) nine

7 What is Captain Wentworth's first name?

8 'That tooth of her's! and those freckles!' Elizabeth is speaking; who is she talking about?

9 How old is Anne when she and Captain Wentworth first meet?

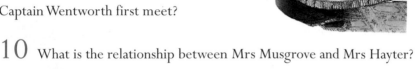

10 What is the relationship between Mrs Musgrove and Mrs Hayter?

11 Dr Shirley is a rector. True or false?

12 Who at the beginning of the novel 'had no fortune'?

13 *Persuasion* has three characters who are naval offices. True or false?

14 Name as many of them as you can.

15 Which characters have a son called Richard?

16 Match these names correctly:

Louisa	Charles	Frederick
Wentworth	Hayter	Musgrove

1　What was the beginning and end of Sir Walter's Elliot's character?

2　'It sometimes happens that a woman is handsomer at twenty-nine than she was ten years before.' Which of the Elliot girls does this refer to?

3　In this illustration by Hugh Thomson, the caption reads, 'Charles spoils the children so.' Who is speaking?

4　'quite the gentleman in all his notions and behaviour.' Who is he?

5　'Thirteen winters' revolving frosts had seen her opening every ball of credit which a scanty neighbourhood afforded.' Who is she?

6　'It's old wonders and new improvements, with the very beautiful line of cliffs stretching out to the east of the town are what the stranger's eye will seek.' Where is it?

7 'You may *perhaps* like the Heroine, as she is almost too good for me.' So said Austen of Anne Elliot but to whom was she writing?

8 Which book is the only one that Sir Walter Elliot ever looks at 'for his own amusement'?

9 Identify all three characters in this C. E. Brock illustration.

In another moment they walked off together

10 'There was no wound, no blood, no visible bruise; but her eyes were closed, she breathed not, her face was like death.' Who is she and what has happened to her?

11 In which county does Captain Wentworth's brother live?

12 Whose brother is the former curate of Monkford?

13 The address is Gay Street; who lives there?

14 'its national importance.' What is significant about these words?

DIFFICULT *Persuasion*

1 What is Sir Walter's date of birth?

2 'a civil, cautious lawyer.' Who is he?

3 When Sir Walter decides to leave Kellynch Hall, what are his three alternatives?

4 Name the actor and actress in this adaptation and date it.

5 At the end of *Persuasion*, Anne has two friends to add to Captain Wentworth's list of friends. Who are they?

6 In which year was *Persuasion* completed?

7 Who has been suggested as the model for Captain Wentworth?

8 Why does Mary not like to send her children to the Great House?

9 Identify the two characters in this picture and say who they are discussing.

10 We are told that Mrs Croft is neither tall nor fat. Which words are used to describe her? Be as precise as you can.

11 'His collar-bone was found to be dislocated.'
(a) Who is he?   (b) Who treats him?

12 At the end of the novel, how much money does Captain Wentworth have?

13 When Anne tells Captain Harville that 'Men have had every advantage of us in telling their own story', which two areas does she then go on to say have been in their domain?

14 Mrs Smith's husband has property. Where is it?

15 Name the person who, at the end of the novel, helps to recover this property.

16 How big is Mrs Croft's blister?

1 What is the significance to the Elliot family of 5 November 1789?

2 Supply the following information about Elizabeth, Sir Walter's wife.
(a) The date of her marriage.
(b) Her father's name and where he was from.
(c) The year in which she died.

3 Complete the following three lines and say who wrote them:

> *'In a private limbo*
> *Where none had thought to look,*
> *Sat a Hampshire gentleman ... '*

4 This is an illustration by Hugh Thomson and its title is a quotation from the novel. Name the three characters portrayed and supply the title – or as close to it as you can.

5 'Anne Elliot was herself; her enthusiasm for the navy, and her perfect unselfishness, reflect her completely.' Who wrote this and to whom?

6 Specify the general revisions made by Austen to Chapters 10, 11 and 12 and identify the extract given below.

'With all this knowledge of Mr E & this authority to impart it, Anne left Westgate Buildings, her mind deeply busy in revolving what she had heard, feeling, thinking, recalling & forseeing everything; shocked at Mr Elliot, sighing over future Kellynch, and pained for Lady Russell, whose confidence in him had been entire. The Embarrassment which must be felt from this hour in his presence! How to behave to him? how to get rid of him? what to do by any of the Party at home? where to be blind? where to be active?'

7 What is the connection between Mrs Croft and Rousseau?

8 Frank Austen considered that he shared certain similarities with Captain Harville. Which three similarities does he particularly refer to?

9 Anne and Captain Benwick discuss two authors when they walk together. Can you name them?

10 'Here it is. I would not burn it.' Who is speaking and what is 'it'?

11 Look at this map of Bath. Can you identify the following locations and say who lives where?

       Marlborough Buildings   Rivers Street   Westgate Buildings

       Mrs Smith   Captain Wallis   Lady Russell

12 Using this map, plot the location of the White Hart and say who stayed there.

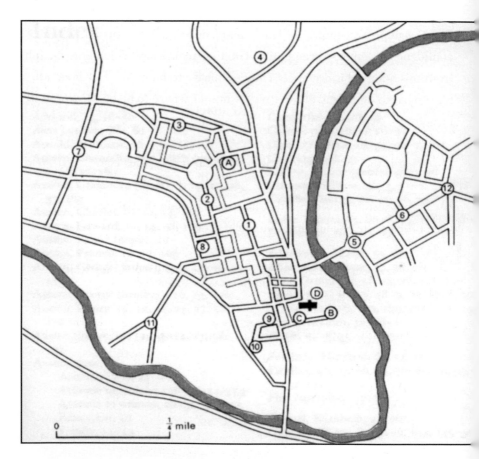

Jane Austen, her Family, her Life and Times

EASY

1   Six.
2   True.
3   George.
4   Clergyman.
5   (c) Hampshire.
6   She didn't marry.
7   False. Cassandra.
8   (b) 8
9   France.
10 A carriage.
11 William Pitt the Younger.
12 (b) Georgian.
13 False. She had one, Cassandra.
14 The French and American Revolutions.
15 A is the earliest, followed by B and then C.
16 George III.
17 (a) Jenny.
18 (c) Four.

MEDIUM

1   Four.
2   He was her nephew.
3   They were both in the Royal Navy.
4   The piano.
5   Schools at Oxford and Reading.
6   Edward, James, Frank, Charles, Henry, George.
7   (a) 25.
8   Bath.
9   It was Jane's last address.
10 Her sister Cassandra.
11 Muslin.
12 Grecian.
13 Jane Austen described by her brother, Henry.
14 A fashionable woman's head dress.
15 A lady's bag.
16 They appeared in the anonymously published novel *Sense and Sensibility* in place of Jane's name.

DIFFICULT

1. Victorian Gothic or Gothic Revival and Classical.
2. Anna.
3. James Edward Austen-Leigh.
4. £140.
5. Having more than one parish.
6. A carriage for hire by those who did not have their own.
7. Addison's Disease.
8. Winchester Cathedral, 1817.
9. He was Jane's favourite poet.
10. James.
11. Walcot.
12. April 1764.
13. The Lloyds, the Lefroys and the Bigg-Withers.
14. Thomas Lefroy.
15. A Spencer jacket.
16. Empire gowns did not have pockets, so a bag was needed.
17. On Jane's tomb.
18. *First Impressions* or the first version of *Pride and Prejudice*.
19. Cadell.

REQUIRING RESEARCH

1. 1809.
2. Elizabeth Hardwick.
3. *A Vindication of the Rights of Woman*.
4. 10 High Street.
5. Jane stopped writing her unfinished novel, *Sanditon*.
6. Anna and Ben Lefroy.
7. Jane's publisher.
8. Near the centre of the north aisle.
9. Three.
10. Her father's, Rev. George Austen.
11. Twelve.
12. Emma Smith.
13. She married Jane's nephew, James Edward.
14. Margaret Carpenter.
15. Anne Mathew.
16. Mary Austen (née Lloyd).
17. '...the involvements and feelings and characters of ordinary life which is to me the most wonderful I have ever met with.'

Locations and Buildings

EASY

1   She was born there.
2   *Northanger Abbey* and *Persuasion*.
3   False. *Persuasion*.
4   (b) Portsmouth.
5   Chawton, Hampshire.
6   True.
7   *Northanger Abbey*.
8   *Mansfield Park*.
9   False. *Sense and Sensibility*.
10 *Persuasion*.
11 True.
12 *Pride and Prejudice*.
13 The parlour at Chawton with Jane's desk.
14 (a) Evelyn.
15 *Emma*.

MEDIUM

1   *Persuasion*.
2   Lyme.
3   *Northanger Abbey*.
4   The Abbey Gateway and Abbey School which Jane attended.
5   Jane visited Great Bookham, which she then used as Box Hill, a setting in *Emma*.
6   *Sense and Sensibility*.
7   The Royal Crescent.
8   *Pride and Prejudice* and *Mansfield Park*.
9   Darcy to Elizabeth.
10 Wiltshire.
11 Steventon Rectory. Anna Lefroy.
12 Catherine's reaction to Northanger Abbey.
13 The Theatre Royal, Bath.
14 Cheltenham.

DIFFICULT

1 The Vyne, a sixteenth-century house near Basingstoke. Jane went there for dances.
2 Godmersham, Kent.
3 Kent and London.
4 Chawton Manor.
5 The Bargate, Southampton. Mrs Austen, Jane, Cassandra and Martha Lloyd moved to Southampton after Mr Austen's death.
6 The seaside.
7 Cheap Street.
8 *Mansfield Park*.
9 4 Sydney Place, Bath. The Austens moved there in 1801.
10 The Austens moved there in 1804 from Sydney Place.
11 *Frederic and Elfrida*.
12 *Lesley Castle*.
13 Winchester.

REQUIRING RESEARCH

1 Revd Tom Fowle died there.
2 Ilchester Gaol.
3 The ruins of Netley Abbey. Jane and her family used to visit it when they were living in Southampton.
4 Steventon.
5 Tom Lefroy visited the Rectory and met Jane there.
6 M. de Feuillide, the husband of one of Jane's cousins.
7 It was the early name of Chawton Cottage, Jane Austen's house.
9 Cassandra, three maids and one manservant. Henry Austen and his wife were staying with her.
10 *Sanditon*.
11 Three acres.
12 Her father rented it from Thomas Knight.
13 In the 1820s because it was no longer thought suitable to house clergy.
14 The Earl of Portsmouth and Lord Bolton. The Austens were invited to both places for balls.
15 Ibthorpe, home of the Lloyd family. Austen visited them there.
16 *Love and Freindship*.

Courtships, Weddings and Marriages

EASY

1 Mr Darcy.
2 Emma and Mr Knightley; Fanny Price and Edmund Bertram; Catherine Morland and Henry Tilney.
3 False. *Emma*.
4 Colonel Brandon.
5 *Persuasion*.
6 Mr Collins, Elizabeth Bennet, *Pride and Prejudice*.
7 (c) *Northanger Abbey*.
8 True.
9 (b) *Lesley Castle*.
10 Jennifer Ehle.
11 False. *The Adventures of Mr Harley*.
12 Marianne.
13 True.
14 Darcy to Elizabeth Bennet.

MEDIUM

1 He proposed to her.
2 *Pride and Prejudice*. Lady Catherine de Burgh is speaking to Mr Collins.
3 Catherine Morland and Henry Tilney.
4 *Mansfield Park*.
5 Anne Elliot, *Persuasion*.
6 Lydia Bennet.
7 *Persuasion*.
8 Mr Darcy, Mr Bingley and Mr Wickham. Wickham.
9 Improver.
10 1. He will set an example of matrimony to his parishioners.
2. It will make him happy.
3. Lady Catherine de Burgh has advised him to marry.
11 False. *Mansfield Park*.
12 rapid; admiration; matrimony *Pride and Prejudice*.
13 Henry Crawford.
14 Miss Bingley.
15 *Love and Freindship*.

DIFFICULT

1 He became engaged to Cassandra.
2 Frances Ward, *Mansfield Park*.
3 James the First.
4 Francis Austen.
5 duly inferior.
6 'A word, a look.'
7 *Lady Susan*.
8 *Evelyn*.
9 Edmund and Fanny, *Mansfield Park*.
10 *Frederic and Elfrida*, *Volume the First*.
11 'a thousand a-year.'
12 Margaret, *Sense and Sensibility*.
13 Elizabeth Elliot, *Persuasion*.
14 Anna had married ten days earlier.
15 Jane Austen in a letter to her niece.

married Benjamin Lefroy on 8 November 1814.

8 *A Collection of Letters*.
9 St George's, George's Street / Hanover Square, London, was very popular for Regency weddings, celebrating a record number of 1,063 in 1816. John James was the architect. Mary Anne Lewis married Disraeli; Harriet Westbrook married Shelley.
10 Henry Austen.
11 agitated; to cry.
12 'that of loving longest, when existence or when hope is gone.'
13 preferred; endured; without; affection.
14 Being in love at first sight.

REQUIRING RESEARCH

1 French. (Eliza Hancock)
2 Fanny Palmer and Charles Austen's.
3 *The Watsons*.
4 Reverend Herbert Hill.
5 John Plumtree.
6 Princess Charlotte's wedding dress, 1816.
7 Austen's niece, Anna, who

ANSWERS *Identify the Novel*

EASY

1 *Pride and Prejudice.*

2 *Emma* and *Persuasion.*

3 False. *Sense and Sensibility.*

4 *Mansfield Park.*

5 True.

6 Mr Collins is in *Pride and Prejudice*; Anne Elliot is in *Persuasion*; Elinor Dashwood is in *Sense and Sensibility.*

7 *Northanger Abbey* and *Mansfield Park.*

8 False. *The Watsons.*

9 *Sense and Sensibility.*

10 (a) *Pride and Prejudice*
(b) *Catharine*
(c) *Northanger Abbey*

11 (c) *Sanditon.*

12 True.

13 (a) Colonel Campbell is in *Emma*; (b) General Tilney in *Northanger Abbey*; (c) Captain Harville in *Persuasion.*

MEDIUM

1 *Sense and Sensibility.*

2 *The History of England.*

3 *Northanger Abbey* and *Persuasion.*

4 *Pride and Prejudice.*

5 *Emma.*

6 *Northanger Abbey.*

7 *Mansfield Park.*

8 *Love and Freindship.*

9 *Sense and Sensibility.*

10 *Persuasion.*

11 *Emma.*

12 *Pride and Prejudice.*

13 *Lesley Castle.*

14 *Sanditon.*

DIFFICULT

1 *Pride and Prejudice* is the 'lop't and crop't' version of *First Impressions*.

2 *The Watsons*.

3 A letter to Cassandra, 17 October 1815.

4 *Volume the First*.

5 *Northanger Abbey*, *Persuasion*, *Emma* and the second edition of *Mansfield Park*. He published them.

6 *Catharine*.

7 *The Visit*.

8 *Lesley Castle*.

9 *Catharine*.

10 *Jack and Eliza*.

11 *The Beautifull Cassandra*.

12 *Frederic and Elfrida*.

13 *Volume the First*.

REQUIRING RESEARCH

1 *Susan / Northanger Abbey*. That it have an early publication.

2 French, Italian, German, music, singing, drawing. A lover. *Lady Susan*.

3 *Scraps, Volume the Second*.

4 *Love and Freindship*.

5 *Sense and Sensibility*.

6 John Murray published 2,000 copies on commission of *Emma*.

7 *The Mystery*.

8 Thomas Egerton of the Military Library, Whitehall published *Sense and Sensibility*, *Pride and Prejudice* and the first edition of *Mansfield Park*.

9 *Mansfield Park*.

10 *Evelyn*.

11 *Sanditon*.

12 The amount Jane was paid for *Pride and Prejudice*.

13 *Emma*. The editors of *The New Monthly Magazine* did not consider it to be a significant novel.

14 It was when Jane began *Mansfield Park*.

Who or What is This?

EASY

1   Cassandra Austen.

2   (c) Edward Ferrars, *Sense and Sensibility*.

3   Jane Bennet and Jane Fairfax.

4   False. Miss Crawford, *Mansfield Park*.

5   (a) Summer walking dress.
      (b) Carriage dress, 1811.
      (c) Evening dress from *Ackermann's Repository*, November 1813.

6   Mrs Bennet.

7   Francis.

8   George III.

9   Anne Elliot's father.

10   Anna Austen Lefroy, Jane's niece. Her parents were James Austen and Anne Mathew.

11   Crawford.

12   Mr Bennet.

13   (a) Fanny Price
      (b) Marianne Dashwood.

14   Martha Lloyd.

15   The Bertrams, *Mansfield Park*.

MEDIUM

1   The Austen family's coat of arms.

2   Her nephew, James Edward Austen-Leigh.

3   Anne Elliot, *Persuasion*.

4   They were family friends and neighbours.

5   Fine. Mrs Allen.

6   Frances (Fanny) Burney 1752–1840 was a novelist, diarist and playwright. Austen read and liked her novels.

7   (a) Mr Tilney.

8   This is by Cassandra Austen and is of Mary I of Scotland. It is from her sister Jane's manuscript *The History of England*.

9   Sir Walter Elliot and Lady Russell.

10   Marianne Dashwood.

11   George Crabbe was one of Austen's favourite writers.

12   Johnson.

13   Mrs Allen and Mr Tilney.

14   (a) Edward; (b) James; (c) Francis.

15   Elizabeth (Bennet), Elizabeth (Elliot), Mary (Crawford) and Mary (Musgrove).

DIFFICULT

1   Oliver Goldsmith. He wrote *The History of England* which Austen parodied.

2   It is the time and date of the death of Jane's father.

3   George, Edward Austen's second son and so her nephew.

4   Stephen Lushington of Norton Court was the MP for Canterbury. He is referred to in a letter written by Jane to Cassandra dated Thursday 14 October 1813.

5   *The Watercolour Portrait of Jane Austen*, by James Stanier Clarke in 1815. It is found in his *Friendship Book*.

6   John Murray.

7   Jane's aunt for shoplifting.

8   Miss Beverley was the heroine of *Cecilia* by Fanny Burney.

9   Jane had written to Crosby enquiring about the manuscript of *Susan*. She used Mrs Ashton Dennis as a pseudonym.

10   Thomas Langlois Lefroy who became Lord Chief Justice of Ireland. He had met Austen when they were both young and in later years told a nephew that his feelings for her had been 'boyish love'.

11   Edward the Fifth.

12   Richardson wrote *The History of Sir Charles Grandison*, which Austen parodied in her early play, *Sir Charles Grandison or the Happy Man, a comedy in six acts*.

13   Jane's mother was a member of the Leigh family and this is the coat of arms of the Barons Leigh.

Who or What is This?

REQUIRING RESEARCH

1 (a) The storming of the Bastille, 14 July 1789. (b) 'Battle of the Nile' by Luny Thomas. The picture depicts Nelson's victory over Napoleon. (c) Laurence Sterne, 1713–68, whose most famous works are his novels *The Life and Opinions of Tristram Shandy, Gentleman* and *A Sentimental Journey Through France and Italy*.

2 Emily St Aubert is found in *The Mysteries of Udolpho* by Ann Radcliffe, which Austen parodies in *Northanger Abbey*.

3 Mr Papillon.

4 Jane Williams.

5 Henry Austen went bankrupt in March 1816.

6 Mr Jeffrey.

7 Anna Lefroy.

8 George Henry Lewes, a critic and philosopher who wrote enthusiastically about Austen's work.

9 John Murray's reader was William Giffard.

10 Mrs Augusta Branston.

11 Mr B. C. Southam.

12 (a) Jane Williams, née Cooper (Jane's cousin). (b) Mrs Lefroy.

13 Mr Clifford.

Pride and Prejudice

EASY

1. False. Elizabeth Bennet.
2. (b) Five.
3. Elizabeth, Jane, Lydia, Kitty (Catherine), Mary.
4. The Lucas family.
5. Colin Firth, Mr Darcy.
6. They are friends.
7. Lydia Bennet.
8. (c) 20.
9. True.
10. It is the Bollywood version, *Bride and Prejudice*.
11. Fitzwilliam.
12. Lydia Bennet.
13. Lady Catherine de Burgh.
14. Mr Collins.

MEDIUM

1. Maria Lucas.
2. Mary and Kitty.
3. Harriet, Colonel Foster's wife.
4. Mrs Reynolds.
5. Two young women travelling by themselves.
6. Mary.
7. 1906.
8. Jane Austen.
9. They both wrote screenplays for adaptations.
10. Lady Catherine de Burgh.
11. Darcy and Mr Bingley.
12. (a) Brenda Blethyn
    (b) Judi Dench
13. Laurence Olivier and Greer Garson.
14. Mr Hurst.

DIFFICULT

1   Thomas Egerton's.

2   Attorney. Meryton.

3   Andrew Davies.

4   Four thousand pounds.

5   Another novel with this title had been published in 1800.

6   Richard Brinsley Sheridan.

7   1796.

8   Elizabeth, Maria Lucas and Sir William Lucas.

9   Aldous Huxley.

10   Jane had just received a copy of the published novel.

11   He is a librarian in the 1940 MGM film.

12   Prunella Scales.

13   Mr Hurst, Bingley's brother-in-law, lives in Grosvenor Street and Elizabeth's uncle and aunt, Mr and Mrs Gardiner, live in Gracechurch Street.

REQUIRING RESEARCH

1   Hunsford, near Westerham, Kent.

2   A. A. Milne. He wrote a stage version of it.

3   Jane discovered the phrase 'pride and prejudice' in this book.

4   A clergyman at Pemberley.

5   Annabella Milbanke.

6   1817.

7   'two speeches are made into one.'

8   J. P. Dent & Co in London; E. P. Dutton & Co in New York.

9   Around 1,500.

10   July 1813.

11   Robert Goldman and George Weiss. Glenn Paxton wrote the music.

12   Hermione Gingold. Mrs Bennet.

13   Jane does not name the regiment in *First Impressions* but the Derbyshire Militia were in Hertford and Ware during the winter of 1794–5.

14   29 January 1813.

Sense and Sensibility

EASY

1   Three.
2   True.
3   Devon.
4   She falls and twists her foot. He carries her home.
5   Mrs Jennings is Lady Middleton's mother.
6   Edward Ferrars; Lucy Steele; Fanny Dashwood.
7   Emma Thompson played Elinor Dashwood.
8   He directed it.
9   One son.
10 (c) Thirteen.
11 (b) Willoughby.
12 Over thirty-five.
13 Elinor Dashwood.
14 Willoughby and Marianne.

MEDIUM

1   Sussex.
2   (a) Robert Ferrars
    (b) John Dashwood
    (c) John Middleton
3   Mr and Mrs Palmer.
4   Mrs Jennings about Marianne.
5   Sir John and Lady Middleton.
6   London.
7   £500.
8   Mr Palmer.
9   Business.
10 Greg Wise, Willoughby; Kate Winslet, Marianne.
11 £250.
12 Somerset.
13 Elinor's.
14 To Delaford.
15 Alan Rickman. Colonel Brandon.

DIFFICULT

1   Three days.
2   The first week in January.
3   As a gentleman who is carrying a gun. Two pointers.
4   Cheerful, agreeable, good-humoured, merry, fat, elderly.
5   Eliza and Colonel Brandon who loved one another but Eliza was forced to marry his brother.
6   Joanna David, Elinor Dashwood, BBC version of 1971.

7   Edward.

8   Robert's income is £1,000 per year. £10,000 is the settlement Mrs Ferrars makes for Edward, which enables him to marry.

9   Edward.

10   Understanding and judgement.

11   1985. Rodney Bennett.

12   When Willoughby takes a lock of Marianne's hair, Margaret sees it; she tells Mrs Jennings what Edward Ferrars' initials are.

REQUIRING RESEARCH

1   Anna, Jane's niece.

2   The film is a contemporary Indian take on *Sense and Sensibility*.
     (a) *I Have Found It*
     (b) Rajiv Menon
     (c) Tamil

3   Conscience.

4   Jane had not told Anna about writing *Sense and Sensibility*. When they were both in the Alton Library, Anna saw the first volume on the counter, picked it up and spoke about it dismissively.

5   Series of English Idylls.

6   30 October 1811.

7   Fifteen shillings. Three volumes.

8   Lady Bessborough.

9   Her lover, Lord Granville Leveson-Gower.

10   The John Dashwoods live in Harley Street; Sir John Middleton in Conduit Street; Mrs Jennings in Berkeley Street.

11   Colonel Brandon.

12   Bartlett Buildings, off Holborn Circus.

13   Only the Steeles are relatively poor and they live away from the others; the remainder, who are wealthy, live close to one other.

14   disagreement; coolness; their husbands.

EASY

1   Woodhouse.
2   The Martins.
3   False. She has a sister.
4   Frank Churchill.
5   She is the school mistress.
6   Jane Fairfax; Harriet Smith; Frank Churchill.
7   Twenty.
8   False. Mr and Mrs Weston.
9   George.
10   (b) Mr Perry.
11   Harriet Smith and Mr Elton.
12   Mr Elton.
13   Isabella, Emma's sister.
14   Gwyneth Paltrow.
15   Miss Taylor's.

MEDIUM

1   Handsome, clever and rich.
2   Hazel.
3   Seventeen or eighteen years.
4   Herself.
5   The Crown Inn.
6   Augusta.
7   Mr Elton.
8   Emma's nephews and nieces.
9   Her mother.
10   She considers that she can have nothing to do with them.
11   They are secretly engaged.
12   Mr Knightley about Harriet Smith.

13   Frank Churchill and Jane Fairfax.
14   Kate Beckinsdale and Mark Strong.
15   False. 1996.
16   Apothecary.

DIFFICULT

1   With the Campbells.
2   The title page of the 1909 edition. C. E. Brock.
3   Miss Hawkins.
4   Mr Elton and Mr Perry.
5   Tea and quadrille.
6   Watercolour. It is full length.
7   Over the mantelpiece.
8   Towards the end of the novel, Jane Fairfax is to go to Mrs Smallridge and care for her three children.
9   Harriet Smith's forthcoming marriage to Robert Martin.
10   Serle's.
11   She is not young, handsome, rich or married.
12   Mrs Elton.
13   '… a pretty little Tunbridge-ware box …'
14   Harriet Smith and Robert Martin in September; Emma and Mr Knightley in October.

15 It was rumoured that they were all seen with a slice of the wedding cake in their hands but Mr Woodhouse would not believe the rumour.

16 'the perfect happiness of the union.'

REQUIRING RESEARCH

1 *The hood-wink'd boy I called to aid,*
Though of his near approach afraid,
So fatal to my suit before.

2 Garrick.

3 Because 'Human nature is so well disposed towards those who are in interesting situations,'

4 Doran Goodwin, 1972.

5 A card game for four players.

6 Isabella, Emma's sister, was almost christened Catherine after her grandmother.

7 Miss Nash, Miss Prince and Miss Richardson. They are teachers and they eat a goose given to Mrs Goddard by Mrs Martin.

8 According to Harriet Smith, Robert Martin has read the first of these books, has never heard of the other two but, since Harriet mentioned them, is determined to read them.

9 'Very little white satin, very few lace veils; a most pitiful business!'

10 (a) the parlour; two
(b) 25 years
(c) eight cows, including two Alderneys and a Welch cow.

11 Robert Martin was twenty-four on 8 June. Harriet Smith's birthday is 23 June.

12 Emma, Harriet, Jane Fairfax and the two Miss Coxes.

13 Maple Grove.

14 Augusta's wealthy brother-in-law from Bristol.

15 John Carson; John Glenister.

Northanger Abbey

EASY

1 Catherine Morland.
2 (a) Ten.
3 John Thorpe.
4 (c) School friends.
5 Henry Tilney; John Thorpe; James Morland.
6 '... conceal it as well as she can.'
7 Susan.
8 (b) Sedentary.
9 Catherine Morland and Isabella Thorpe.
10 Isabella is older by four years.
11 Henry Tilney.
12 True.
13 He is a clergyman.
14 False. This is a description of Miss Tilney.

MEDIUM

1 Fifteen.
2 Mrs Thorpe.
3 Mr and Mrs Morland.
4 For his gout.
5 Dancing and marriage.
6 She is the author of *The Mysteries of Udolpho*, a novel that Catherine Morland is reading.
7 '... the pangs of disappointed love.'
8 Eleanor Tilney.
9 From fifteen to seventeen.
10 Pulteney Street.
11 John Thorpe.
12 Henry Tilney.
13 Four weeks.
14 Twenty miles.

DIFFICULT

1 'John was at Oxford, Edward at Merchant Taylors' and William at sea'.

2 Fifty guineas.

3 Henry Austen, after her death.

4 Dorothy.

5 Four weeks at Bath and four days at Fullerton.

6 Udolpho; Pulteney; Upper Rooms.

7 A narrow escape from John Thorpe and a request to dance by Henry Tilney.

8 1798.

9 Googie Withers.

10 Pope, Gray, Thomson and Shakespeare.

11 The recommendation of 'parental tyranny' or the reward of 'filial disobedience'.

12 *Castle of Wolfenbach, Clermont, Mysterious Warnings, Necromancer of the Black Forest, Midnight Bell, Orphan of the Rhine* and *Horrid Mysteries*.

13 Miss Andrews.

14 Ignorant and uninformed.

15 If everyone were to drink a bottle of liquor a day.

REQUIRING RESEARCH

1 To 'bear about the mockery of woe.'

2 '… waste its sweetness on the desert air.' Gray.

3 To take a pin out of her sleeve.

4 Nine shillings.

5 That she is unsure, has never really thought about it, she likes something in between; she prefers brown, not fair, but not too dark.

6 John Thorpe and Catherine Morland. 'A famous good thing this marrying scheme.'

7 Between two dresses, 'her spotted and her tamboured muslin.'

8 Embroidered. A tambour is a small frame used for embroidery.

9 *Sir Charles Grandison*.

10 That it is 'an amazing horrid book' and that Miss Andrews could not finish the first volume.

11 Sam is a friend of John Thorpe's and they are planning to get a house in Leicestershire for the next season.

12 Sam Fletcher's.

13 'chosen a wife with less sense than his family expected.'

14 General Tilney in a chaise and four. Ten o'clock in the morning.

15 They are by Shakespeare and Catherine read them as a young girl.

Mansfield Park

EASY

1. True.
2. They are sisters.
3. (a) Mrs Norris.
4. (b) Ten.
5. Julia Bertram.
6. William, Fanny's brother.
7. Fanny Price; Mary Crawford; Edmund Bertram.
8. A pony.
9. True.
10. Four.
11. False. She preferred *Pride and Prejudice*.
12. Introvert.
13. A pug.

MEDIUM

1. Henry Crawford.
2. Their education.
3. Tom, Edmund, Maria and Julia.
4. Dr Grant.
5. Sir Thomas Bertram.
6. Antigua.
7. Henry Crawford about Fanny Price.
8. Mr Rushworth about Henry Crawford.
9. Edmund Bertram and Mary Crawford.
10. Henry Crawford.
11. Jane Austen.
12. (c) Less than twenty.
13. Mr Rushworth.
14. Amelia.

Difficult

1. Mansfield Park and then to a small house, owned by Sir Thomas, in the village.
2. Miss Lee.
3. Fanny Price, Miss Bertram, Mr Rushworth and Mr Crawford.
4. Susan.
5. The East Room.
6. Ten pounds.
7. Mrs Fraser. Margaret.
8. In the little white attic near the nurseries.
9. 1908.
10. Amber. Sicily.
11. Five foot eight.
12. Hedgerows.
13. Agreeable.
14. Noise, disorder and impropriety.

Requiring Research

1. Mr and Mrs Cooke.
2. Harold Pinter. He played Sir Thomas Bertram in a television adaptation.
3. The Parsonage.
4. Sylvestra Le Touzel.
5. 'It would give me the greatest pleasure, but that I am this moment going to dance.'
6. Miss Pope.
7. Tintern Abbey, a cave in Italy and a moonlit lake in Cumberland.
8. 'My own sister as a wife, Sir Thomas Bertram as a husband.'
9. Arcturus and the Bear.
10. Both sisters want to be seated next to Henry Crawford in the carriage he is driving. Julia is chosen to do so by Mrs Grant.
11. A starling.
12. *A Sentimental Journey Through France and Italy*.
13. Tom Bertram initially has both the part of Anhalt and the Butler to play. However, he feels unable to play Anhalt and so Charles Maddox is chosen to take the role in his place.

Persuasion

EASY

1   Two.
2   (c) 40.
3   (a) Somerset.
4   Bath and Lyme Regis.
5   Sir Walter Elliot.
6   (b) Eight.
7   Frederick.
8   Mrs Clay.
9   Nineteen.
10 They are sisters.
11 True.
12 Captain Wentworth.
13 False. There are four.
14 Captain Benwick, Admiral Croft, Captain Wentworth, Captain Harville.
15 Mr and Mrs Musgrove.
16 Louisa Musgrove; Charles Hayter; Frederick Wentworth.

MEDIUM

1   Vanity.
2   Elizabeth.
3   Mary, his wife.
4   Admiral Croft.
5   Elizabeth Elliot.
6   Lyme.
7   Fanny Knight.
8   The Baronetage.
9   Anne, Mr Elliot and Captain Wentworth.
10 Louisa Musgrove. She fell from the Cobb, in Lyme.
11 Shropshire.
12 Captain Wentworth's.
13 Admiral Croft.
14 They are the final words of *Persuasion*.

DIFFICULT

1. 1 March 1760.
2. Mr Shepherd.
3. London, Bath or another country house.
4. Ciaran Hinds and Amanda Root. 1995.
5. Lady Russell and Mrs Smith.
6. 1816.
7. Frank, Jane's brother.
8. Because their grandmother gives them so many sweet things to eat that they come back irritable and sick.
9. Anne and Mrs Smith. They are discussing Mr Elliot.
10. Squareness, uprightness and vigour of form.
11. Mary's oldest son Charles. Mr Robinson, the apothecary.
12. Twenty-five thousand pounds.
13. Education and the pen.
14. The West Indies.
15. Captain Wentworth.
16. 'the size of a three-shilling piece.'

ANSWERS

REQUIRING RESEARCH

1   Lady Elliot had a stillborn son on that day.

2   (a) 15 July 1784;
(b) James Stevenson of South Park, Gloucestershire;
(c) 1800.

3   'Reading of a book.
It was called *Persuasion*,'
Written by Rudyard Kipling.

4   Captain Wentworth, Anne and Mrs Musgrove. '... he attended to her large fat sighings ... .'

5   Mrs Barrett to Edward Austen-Leigh.

6   The tenth chapter was largely rewritten, the eleventh chapter was new and the original eleventh chapter became, after some small changes, chapter twelve. The extract is the opening lines of Chapter 10, as originally written by Austen.

7   Mrs Croft's first name is Sophy and Sophie is a character in Rousseau's *Emile*.

8   '... his domestic habits, tastes and occupation'.

9   Walter Scott and Lord Byron.

10   Mrs Smith. A letter written to her husband by William Elliot.

11   Captain Wallis lives at Marlborough Buildings (7); Lady Russell lives at Rivers Street (3); Mrs Smith lives near Westgate Buildings (10).

12   (9) The Musgroves.

ACKNOWLEDGEMENTS

Page 14 © Hampshire County Council.
Page 25 photograph © Colin Bates.
Page 27 © 2008 Associated Newspapers Ltd.
Page 36 (top) © 2008 The British Library.
Page 52 (right) © National Portrait Gallery, London.
Pages 67, 76, 77, 81, 83 and 92, BBC Archives.